WORDS

WORDS

Suddenly, from On High!

EDDIE CURRIE

RESOURCE *Publications* · Eugene, Oregon

WORDS
Suddenly, from On High!

Resource Publications
An Imprint of Wipf and Stock Publishers
199 W. 8th Ave., Suite 3
Eugene, OR 97401

www.wipfandstock.com

PAPERBACK ISBN: 978-1-6667-3806-3
HARDCOVER ISBN: 978-1-6667-9828-9
EBOOK ISBN: 978-1-6667-9829-6

03/08/22

CONTENTS

PREFACE

Words, suddenly, from on high
Like water dropping into a still clear pool
Causing ripples, unexpected
Calmness suddenly affected
The status quo changing
Stillness rearranging
Words from on high]

PREFACE

To date I have written over 600 poems in the course of some twenty-five years and have now had the opportunity, in the middle of self-isolation and the coronavirus pandemic, to review these and put them into some sort of order. Here are just some of them!

I never thought that I would write so many poems. They have been written in an amazing array of situations and feelings— some up and some down, some critical and some not and at different seasons and different events! It was an indicator to me, given the sheer volume of poems that then came, that we have no idea as to what God can unlock and do in us when we have a willing heart. My poems have been written about many things—about my family, and my circumstances, and many are written about my wider (Christian) family and about where I have stood in my Christian experience (good and bad)!

It has been very revealing, and very humbling, reading some of them again and seeing where God has taken me over the years since I became a Christian. The poetry writing has been for about half of that time—it came very unexpectedly but in many ways it has been a way of journaling, of writing a diary of sorts, and has been both very therapeutic, and useful, to me!

I hope that, however and whenever they are published, they will be a blessing, and a challenge, to many! They certainly have been a blessing to me!

For him and his glory!
May I live God-ward not Ed-ward!

Eddie Currie
(Newtownards, Northern Ireland)

ALL THIS FOR ME

All this for me
How can that be
The innocent punished
I, the guilty, go free
All this for me
Jesus has died
The just for the unjust
But God satisfied

All this for me
A victory won
A cry «It is finished»
From God's only Son
All this for me
Such wonderful love
Undeserved favour
From God up above

All this for me
Christ's blood was shed
My sins and the sins
Of the world on Him laid
All this for me
So I bow the knee
In worship to Jesus
Who gave all for me

A NEW THING

(Isaiah 43v18,19)

Remember not the former things
Do not dwell on the past
Behold I will do a new thing
Something that will last!

Springing up within you
Can you not see it come?
I am making a way in the desert
In the wasteland, rivers run

Where no rivers before ever ran
Creating a completely new way
And carrying life-giving water
And refreshment day after day

Am I ready to receive it?
Whatever the new thing will be?
Ready to do the will of God
Following Him, not 'me'

A SAFE ARRIVAL

Cattle and sheep on the runway
Donkeys at the baggage claim
Camels standing at the taxi rank
Waiting for an incoming plane
Shepherds on the tarmac
A shining star in view
Royal limos on the ring-road
The local hotels all full

Angels on the tannoy
Visitors from afar
All waiting for a VIP
A celebrity; a star!
Just what would he look like?
Would he wear a crown?
A really royal personage!
Red carpet on the ground

Inward bound! He's coming!
His call sign heard so clear
The message from the tower
He's landing! He is here!
As everyone stood watching
The anticipation grew
But at Bethlehem City Airport
No plane came into view

He hadn't come—or had he?
No incoming flight had made it
The expected king did not arrive
As the arrivals board had stated
But just on the edge of the airport
In a dirty equipment shed
Shepherds and wise men all stood round
Where a mother her baby had laid

It was dark and cold and frosty that night
Not good for a baby's survival
But all who saw him gave glory to God
And gave thanks for a safe arrival!
The King had come—as scripted!
But not as people had thought
Gold, frankincense and myrrh, gifted
To a baby—a king—God

BANANAS AND BRICKS

You can't build a house with bananas
They're not the things to be used
They're "banana-shaped," not "brick-shaped"
And certainly easily bruised!

Bananas start off yellow
But yellow they really don't last
They quickly turn black and go squashy
And certainly degenerate fast!

Imagine a house of bananas
It sure wouldn't last very long
No matter how well you stuck them
The building wouldn't be very strong!

God is building His church with people
Are they good material to use?
So often "me-shaped," not "Christ-shaped"
And they're certainly easily bruised!

They don't always stick well together
Don't always fit in where they should
Often have the consistency of bananas
Instead of stone, brick, and wood!

So, when you see a banana
Here's a good question to moot!
Am I useful to God in His building
Or am I as useful as fruit?

BATTERED AND BRUISED

Battered and bruised
Slapped on the face
Reviled and abused
Dying in disgrace
Spat upon
Flogged
Hammered. . ..and nailed!
In the eyes of the world
Jesus had failed!

Born in a stable
Then having to flee
Avoiding persecution
As a refugee
No status
Low profile
Nothing to bring
Hardly a good pedigree
For becoming a king!

A travelling preacher
No money; no bed
Misunderstood; ridiculed
But raising the dead!
Healing
Sharing
Preaching of love

And a kingdom to covet
Not on earth—but above!

A baby in a manger
A felon on a cross
A man who was penniless
No profit—just loss!
Yet Jesus was different
He was God became man
From everything—to nothing!
That was God's plan

From kingship
To servanthood
From a throne
To a grave
Jesus became nothing
A world to save!

BE GOD'S MAN

No matter what the world may offer
Don't try to follow the crowd—**Be God's man!**

No matter where in the world you go
You should always seek to be—**In God's place!**

No matter what in the world you do
Make sure that you are always—**Doing God's work!**

No matter what the world expects
You should always strive to follow—**In God's way!**

Written in an old Bible belonging to my Grandmother:

> *Be God's Man,*
> *In God's place,*
> *Doing God's work,*
> *In God's Way.*
> —Hudson Taylor

BORN THERE IN BETHLEHEM

(Tune—Meekness and Majesty)

Born there in Bethlehem
Died in Jerusalem
Starting in a manger
And ending on a cross
Into the world he came
For my sins, took the blame
Jesus of Nazareth
Bearing my shame

Living in poverty
Moving in history
Starting with nothing
And then ending with less
Across the world he walked
Of love and grace he talked
Jesus of Nazareth
Has salvation brought

Dying in agony
Crucified on a tree
Becoming sin for me
There on a cross
For the world, took the fall
On him we now must call
Jesus of Nazareth
Was given for all

BROKEN BOTTLES

Broken bottles
Rubber tyres
Polystyrene
Splintered wire
Twisted metal
Rusting tins
Shattered vases
Empty bins
Cardboard boxes;
Paper bags
Plastic bottles
Dirty rags
Rubbish, garbage
This and more
Surplus material to the core

Worthless
But it's what I so often send to you, Lord
Debris and refuse
And so much rubble
All I seem to send is wood, hay and stubble
So little that you can use, Lord

How can you do anything through me?

BY GRACE ALONE

By grace alone
And love for me
It took my Lord
To Calvary
And there He died
My sin to own
I've been redeemed
By grace alone

Through faith alone
It will suffice
It was enough
Christ's sacrifice
I'll look to Him
The world disown
And follow Christ
Through faith alone

In Christ alone
My only aim
To put Him first
And love His name
Nothing in me
His blood atones
I now have all
In Christ alone

By grace alone (x2)
Through faith alone
I'll put my trust
In Christ alone

CAN I FOLLOW IN HIS STEPS?

Can I follow in His steps
The example Jesus gives
Can I follow in the way
Of Jesus, and for Him live?

Can I follow in His steps
His will, my daily food
Asking this question in all things
What would Jesus do?

I don't always follow in His steps
But do what I think is right
When God's will for me each day is
To walk by faith, not sight

It's not easy to follow in His steps
And do what Jesus would will
But it's the only way for Christians
After two thousand years it's still

What Jesus says to disciples
Come; come and follow me
And I will make you fishers of men
In a troubled, fish-filled sea

We should always follow in His steps
Be salt and light on the earth

Follow the Master; make a difference
And shine for all we're worth

"follow in his steps. . ." 1 Peter 2v21

COME SEE A MAN WHO KNEW ME

(John 4v29)

Come see a man who knew me
Better than I knew myself
Who knew my past; my sinning
All that I'd done—but yet

He said He would give me water
Of everlasting life
And said I would never thirst again
Was not this the Christ?

Come see a man who told me
All I ever did
He looked at me with sorrow
And I could see God in Him

How could He really know me?
Know what's in my heart
But God He was—and saw me
My life in every part

DO I LOOK LIKE MY FATHER?

(2 Cor 6v18)

Do I look like my father?
Do I really look like Him?
In his looks; his voice; his manner
Both outwardly and within

When people see me, do they say
He's definitely his father's son?
Do they clearly see in my life
A "mirror image" son

When they see me coming
Do they look me up and down
And say "there's a family likeness"?
In his voice you can hear the sound

Of his Father's speech, and influence
In all that he says and does
He's a good son; he's just like his Father
He's his double and that's because

He follows his Father's example
He wants his Father's "well done"
He oh so wants to please his Dad
And to be a faithful son"

(Rom 8v14–17)

EILEEN

Her name is Eileen, she lives in the Glen
An estate on the north side of town
Six children she has but not all to one man
And her life is getting her down.

The youngest is two; the eldest fourteen
In between, like steps in a stair
The pressure so great there's no way she can cope
She is in the depths of despair.

Two at home, all through the day
One of them crying all night
Three at the primary and one at the grammar
But nobody knows of her plight.

She's oh so lonely and needs good advice
On how to sort out her life
And practical help is needed as well
To look after her family right.

At her wit's end; what can she do
She's eating tablets like sweets
Not enough money; no-one who cares
And struggling to make ends meet.

The Oxfam Shop! War on Want!
The charities are doing their bit

The Sally Army! Social Services!
But where do the churches fit?

They send out missionaries all over the world
And its right, they should so send
But they forget the first part of the Great Commission
To start at "Jerusalem"

There are many "Eileens" around this world
Do we even know that they're there
How can we reach them; give them help
And show them that Jesus cares?

GOD HAS PROMISED

(to the tune "Jesus loves me")

God has promised us each day
He will help in every way
When we need Him He is there
If we come to Him in prayer

Yes, God has promised
Yes, God has promised
Yes, God has promised
The Bible tells us so

When the clouds are dark above
God will always show His love
He is faithful and we know
He'll give grace to us below

Chorus

If we're lost and on our own
God will guide us safely home
We don't ever need to fear
God our Father's always near

Chorus

God has promised, it is true
He will bless both me and you

Jesus is the only way
We can trust in Him today

Chorus

GOD KNOWS!

Feeling lonely, sad, depressed?
God knows!
Feeling pressured, stretched and stressed?
God knows!

No matter how you feel today
Unable to read God's word, or pray
God wants to be your help and stay!
God knows!

Sometimes impossible to lift your head?
God knows!
Perhaps even wishing you were dead?
God knows!

But don't give up, and don't give way
You're not the first to feel that way
Just hold on to Jesus, come what may!
He knows!

Will I ever be able to cope today?
God knows!
Who is going to help me in a positive way?
God knows!

Whatever I do, wherever I go
God always seeks His love to show
Sometimes only through trials I can grow!
God knows!

GOD WITH US

God with us; God's own Son
God as a baby and shepherds come
With angel hosts the worship swells
God with us; Immanuel

God with us; God came down
Wise men came and bowed to the ground
To a child on whom salvation depends
God with us; Immanuel

God with us; Immanuel
God incarnate; with us to dwell
God made flesh as the Bible tells
Jesus our Immanuel

GOD'S NOT FINISHED WITH ME YET

God's not finished with me yet
There's still too far to go!
Shaping me; and changing me
Moulding me; re-making me
Guiding me, step by step

God's not finished with me yet
He has much more work to do
Pushing me; pruning me
Filling; fine-tuning me
My ordered world needs upset

God's not finished with me yet
There's still too much of me!
My wants; my desires
My coldness; my fires
Submission is hard to accept

God's not finished with me yet
But resistance is what I do best!
Digging in; holding on
Not letting go; not letting God
Will I look back with regret?

God's not finished with me yet
«New things,» not the past, is His goal
Transforming me; renewing me
Refreshing me; improving me
God's definitely not finished with me yet!

GROW IN GRACE

(listening to a message by Bishop Ken Clarke
@ Kingdom Come, Belfast—2 February 2010)
(2 Peter 3v18)

Grow in grace and in the knowledge
Of Jesus Christ; as Savior and Lord
Get out of the boat; walk on the water
Look to Jesus; don't stay on board   Sailing
Through the hard times; and «Christ denials»
Through the storms; and «stomach churning" trials
Through all the tossing of your life's vessel
Fix your eyes on Christ!

Grow in grace and in the knowledge
Of Jesus Christ; as Savior and Lord
Run the race that's set before you
Keep up the pace; stay on the road   Running
Through the miles; and «weary turnings»
Through the pain; and "grace muscle" burning
Through the tiredness; and «finish line" yearning
Fix your eyes on Christ!

Grow in grace and in the knowledge
Of Jesus Christ; as Savior and Lord
Learn to love Him; learn to follow
Seek to be like Him; know Him as Lord   Learning
Through the flowing; and «grace bestowing»

Through the sowing; and «God's love showing»
Through the growing; and «Jesus knowing»
Fix your eyes on Christ!

HIS BLOOD IS SPILT

His blood is spilt
His body broken
So often these words
In church are spoken
Yet so much is behind them
So much is implied
That we take it for granted
That Jesus has died

The light of the world
Extinguished and lost
The Saviour of all
Yet nailed to a cross
And the hands he had made
And the tree he created
Were all involved
In that death so hated

If he died to save me
Why himself could he not save
If he took all my sin
Why did he go to the grave
That it was all over
That was him finished
He died and was buried
A life so unblemished

But thankfully, unbelievably
He rose from the grave
And conquered the end of life
For me he had saved
By giving his life for me
Over death he was winning
By defeating the grave
It was a new beginning

By his life and his sacrifice
His example was stunning
God gave himself for me
A prodigal running
To my father and recognising
I needed his grace
That I needed his forgiveness
I wanted his embrace

He gave up his only son
As a ransom for me
Jesus died on the cross
That I might go free

HIS BODY WAS BROKEN

His body was broken
His blood flowed free
As Jesus hung there
On a cross just for me
Nails hammered through Him
A spear in His side
Such love; such indignity
And God crucified

His blood was sufficient
His sacrifice enough
So much accomplished
By Lord Jesus for us
How can we then reject Him?
How can we know?
What it meant for the Savior
To die for us so

His supper is special
His table is free
To all those who love Him
Who to Him bow the knee
How can we neglect it?
How can we forget?
That so much was accomplished
When Christ paid our debt

HOLY SPIRIT COME

Holy Spirit come
And fan the flame
That flickers in my heart
This light that fades

Holy Spirit lead
Me on the road
The way that seems unclear
With heavy load

Holy Spirit change
My heart within
Stripping out my self life
Help me to live

Holy Spirit cleanse
Me deep inside
Help me deal with selfishness
Sin and pride

Holy Spirit fill
For God, not self
Help me pledge allegiance
To Christ—none else

I'M OUTTA HERE!

Luke 15v11–32

I'm outta here! I've had enough
Of this rural living and farming stuff
I want what I'm due, what's owed to me
I'll take my half and then I'm free
To leave this place—go where I want
Live how I like! Yes, now's my chance
To see new things—new friends too, I reckon
A whole new world before me beckons

I scraped the farm from off my boots
I left my home—I took the loot
But I'm stuck here now—the going's tough
This urban living and glamour stuff
Has drained me dry, I've nothing left
My so-called friends have failed the test
As my money went so they went too
I'm now in the red, I'm feeling blue

I do have some friends of the 'piggy' kind!
I eat their food, it's all I can find
Just what can I do? I've nowhere to go
I'd be better off if I went home!
My father loved me. Might love me still
I'd be better off going back to him
I've nothing here—no longer rich
These pigswill sandwiches I'll never miss!

I'm gonna go home, I'm gonna say
Dad, make me a servant in your house today
He might say "yes" He might say "no"
But until I try it I'll never know
You'll never believe it! Dad saw me coming
Ran to meet me—it was really something!
A robe, new shoes. A ring, fillet steak!
My father gave me all for love's sake

Amazing love he had for me
My brother did not! What thought he?
If only he could he would have shoved me
Back into the pigsty but Dad still loved me
My selfish heart took me away
But Dad didn't give up and love found a way!
His love was perfect—he cared for me
His son, once lost—was found, you see!

IN THIS BREAD AND ITS BREAKING

In this bread and its breaking
Though only a token
I am taken back
To a body broken
A man on a cross
Dying for me
Taking my punishment
That I might go free

In this cup and its drinking
I take the wine
Thinking of Christ's blood
Simply a sign
Of a man on a cross
Dying for me
Giving His life's blood
A ransom for me

I WAS CAUGHT IN THE MIDDLE OF MY SIN

(John 8v1–11)

I was caught in the middle of my sin
Not worried about doing the wrong thing
The door burst open and some men charged in
Grabbed me and pushed me through the dust and the din

Fingers pointing at me and accusing eyes
In my shame and my sin; I had nowhere to hide
Into the temple they drew me in front of the crowd
Their shouts and their jeers echoing loud

People crying "We found her in the very act
Of adultery," I was thinking "It takes two, that's a fact"
In front of me a man sat; another accuser
Just what I needed—another abuser

But this man seemed different; he just sat there in silence
Bent over and started writing; would he stop the violence
I was standing alone; I watched him and waited
To see what he would do, with breath that was bated

He started to speak ; I strained to hear
"Is there anyone who stands without sin here?"
'Whoever is sinless let him cast the first stone
In a very few moments my accusers were gone

No-one now left to accuse me of sin
All were now gone but me—and him!
"Woman, where are they now the ones who condemned"
It was clear to me he was not like them

Words of wisdom indeed but there was something more
"Go your way and sin no more"

I'M SPECIAL (NEW VERSE)

I'll follow Him each day and serve Him
For I want to give Him everything I have, and
God calls me just to live like Jesus
and to be like Him in everything I do

Thank you, Jesus
Thank you, Lord
For showing me your love
And giving grace I need every day
Help me share that love with all
And tell a sinful world
That Jesus died for them

I'M WALKING IN THE DARKNESS

I'm walking in the darkness; and I don't
  understand
Why there isn't any light here; is this
  what God has planned?

I'm stumbling in the darkness; I cannot
  easily stand
But I don't need to worry at all; for Jesus
  holds my hand

He holds me tight; I need not fear
Through wrong and right; He's always near
By faith, not sight; I'll persevere
I'm never on my own!

IN FOLLOWING

In following
In caring
In walking
In sharing
In working
In living
In serving
In giving
In waiting
In running
In seeking
In coming
In standing
In doing
In hearing
In moving
May Jesus be thought of
May I follow the Son
In everything, faithful
His will always done

Jesus—only Jesus!

IN THE DARK OF THE NIGHT

In the dark of the night
And the midst of the storm
There are arms that hold me
And keep me from harm

No matter how troubled
And angry the sea
With Jesus beside me
I know I'll have peace

In the dazzle of wanting
Always thirsting for more
Of what the world offers
Just why is my heart sore?

God says «Don't be troubled»
Believe only in me
Simply look unto Jesus
For in Him, you'll be free

In the draw of temptation
And the down of despair
With no-one to hold me
God says «I'll be there»

No matter how pressed
And troubled inside
He will never leave me
He'll be by my side

IRELAND

Who will spread the good news of Jesus
Throughout this land of ours?
Where people fight and people kill
Led by satanic powers!

Chorus
How shall they hear?
How shall they know?
Are we ready to pray?
Are we ready to go?
How shall they hear of heaven and hell?
Only if we speak!
Only if we tell!

Men full of hate and full of sin
Across this land so fair
The land of saints and scholars once
Now so much in need of prayer!

This land so beautiful, so dear to us
This Ireland, so green and proud
Now divided by hate, divided by sin
With pride and arrogance endowed!

ISAIAH 53

Like a tender shoot
Out of the dry ground
In weakness and humility
In him is found
No beauty, no majesty
Like no other before him
Nothing in his appearance
That we should desire him

Despised and rejected
Again and again
A man of suffering
Familiar with pain
He took up our suffering
He was pierced for our sin
Crushed for our iniquities
Bringing peace within

Like wandering sheep
Doing our own thing
Our sins and transgressions
The Lord laid on him
Like a lamb to the slaughter
From his mouth, no breath
A grave with the wicked
With the rich in his death

God's will to crush him
And to see him suffer
Make His life an offering
For sin and for me
Bearing my iniquities
Bearing my shame
Numbered with the sinful
Oh, praise to his name

Bearing the sin of many
He prayed out «Lord forgive»
Poured out his life as a ransom
And prayed that they might live

JESUS, CAN YOU HEAR ME?

Jesus, can you hear me?
I'm calling to you
I'm in trouble; I'm sinking
Don't know what to do

Lord—speak to the waves
Speak to the wind
In the storms of my life
Say «Peace be still»

Jesus, I can't hear you!
Your voice is so faint
I'm trying hard to listen
To live just by faith

Lord—speak clearly to me
May I know your will
In this noise and this turmoil
Hear you saying «be still»

Jesus I do hear you
Speaking to me
Leading me; guiding
Your way to see

Lord, speak to my heart
Help me fulfil
Your purpose; your plan
And hear you say «still»

JESUS DIED INSTEAD OF ME

Jesus died instead of me
He was crucified; I was set free
My sin was so great
My crime was hateful
When he died in my place
I was extremely grateful
About his death I have thought hard and long
Why did he die when he had done no wrong?
I was tried; so was he
I was found guilty but then was set free!

Why did he do it?
No matter how you view it
He did not have to die
He took my place
I can still see his face
On a wooden cross lifted high
Some people called him «Son of the Father»
My name's the same, but I would rather
Let you guess it—yes, it's Barabbas!
The man for whom Jesus died

JESUS ONLY; MY DESIRE

Jesus only; my desire
Jesus only; Lord, light that fire
That makes me want to lift you higher
Jesus, only Jesus.

Jesus only; Him alone
Jesus only; Lord on the throne
May I look to Him; the world disown
Jesus, only Jesus.

Jesus only; Lord to me
Jesus only; only He
Can bring me life and joy and peace
Jesus, only Jesus

Jesus only; the world neglects
Jesus only; the world forgets
And only gives when it can get
Not Jesus; never Jesus!

Jesus only; gave His all
Jesus only; hear Him call
"Come unto me; come lean upon"
Jesus, only Jesus

Jesus only; died for me
Jesus only; on that tree
Dying there to set me free
Jesus, only Jesus

Jesus only; loved so much
Jesus only; dying once
That's all it took; it was enough
Jesus, only Jesus

JOHN 3V16

In John chapter three and verse sixteen
The most beautiful words can there be seen
A message for the world
A message to promote
For the lost—a way forward
For the hopeless, hope!
For God so loved a world that was lost
He gave his only Son

LORD JESUS, YOU LOVED ME

(To the tune «Annie's Song»)

Lord Jesus, you loved me
And you gave yourself for me
Lord, you died there on Calvary
And you saved me from sin
Then you rose on the third day
Over death you have conquered
In heaven you're reigning
But will come again

Lord, let me worship
Let me praise you forever
May I glorify Jesus in all that I do
May I lift up my heart, Lord
In all reverence and wonder
At all of your works, Lord
In heaven and earth

Oh Lord, let me serve you
Let me give my life to you
Let me tell others of you
And of your wondrous love
Let me always be faithful
Let me watch for your coming
So come then, Lord Jesus
My Savior and King

LORD, WE REMEMBER AGAIN

(Isaiah 53)

Lord, we remember again
The Man of Sorrows; rejected by men
No beauty; no majesty
Smitten by God
On Jesus the sins of the world were laid

Led like a lamb to the blade
Going in silence; not a word said
No anger; no rebellion
Submissive to God
Walked Jesus to Calvary; the Lamb who was slain

We are like sheep gone astray
Lost in the wilderness of our own way
No wisdom; no clarity
Drifting from God
Needing direction from Jesus the Way

Jesus has died for us all
Smitten, afflicted, forsaken by God
He poured out his lifeblood
An offering to God
Our sins now forgiven—condemnation gone!

LORD—IF I'M IN THE WAY

Lord

If I'm in the way—push me aside!

If I'm putting myself first—push me down!

If I'm holding back—push me forward!

If I'm pushing myself forward—push me back!

LORD, CAN YOU USE ME?

Lord, can you use me?
What can I do?
That is less about me
And more about you!

Lord, will you take me?
And use me today
To reach others for Jesus
Who alone is the way!

Lord, will you guide me?
Show me your will
May I serve you with gladness
Your purpose fulfil!

Lord, will you fill me
Cleanse me within
Help me be holy
More resistant to sin!

Lord, will you break me?
Sort out my pride
Humble me further
My self life denied!

LOVE SO AMAZING

Love so amazing
Grace so free
Peace so tranquil
Faith—to see

Joy so surprising
Truth so clear
Mercy unwarranted
Freedom from fear

Comfort in sorrow
Holiness pure
Strength so unlimited
Hope that is sure

Gifts that are given
By God to me
Goodness unending
Faithfulness seen

MERCY AND GRACE

(Hebrews 4v16)

We can boldly seek God's face
Look for mercy and for grace
These two things we need each day
To help us walk the Christian way

We must come in Jesus' name
He knows the weakness of our frame
Every day it's still the same
We can come and come again

Grace to help in time of need
Mercy obtained for sinful deed
Praise God we can ask these in Jesus' name
And boldly come each day the same

MY SHEPHERD

He loved me; cared for me
Knew me so well
Looked out for me; helped me
Lifted me when I fell

Searched for me
And found me
Put His arms around me

Got me home
In safety
Back in the fold placed me

Healed my wounds
Soothed me
In his love
Moved me

To pastures new
And fed me
By quiet waters, He led me

Looked out for me; helped me
Wanted my increase
He loved me; and cared for me
Giving me peace

OLD FASHIONED LANGUAGE

Old fashioned language
Old fashioned clothes
Why do we use them?
God only knows!
Old fashioned singing
Years out of date
Are all these approaches
Deterrents to grace?

We live in the present
Why then live in the past?
When presenting the Savior
Do people just laugh?
At our well-meaning attitudes
But meaningless ways
Of sharing our Saviour
Through an old-fashioned haze

We should look to God daily
Be ready to hear
What God is saying
Is it coming through clear?
We must be relevant, salt-like
Bright lights in the world
Living each day like Jesus
Showing something of God

When people look at me
What do they see?
When they look at my face
Do they see only me?
Or do they see Jesus
Even a glimpse
Am I anything like Him
Is my self-life eclipsed?

ONLY A LITTLE BABY

Only a little baby, in a dirty cattle stall,
How could a baby change the world,
This little child so small?
No tinsel in the stable, or the usual Christmas things,
But presents, gold and frankincense,
And myrrh, from Eastern kings.

They bowed down to a baby, an infant, soft and warm,
A king like them, yet not the same,
He was God in human form.
A helpless little baby, in surroundings bleak and bare,
The King of Kings, from heaven came,
Sent by a God who cared.

He left His throne in heaven, He left a palace too,
He left the praise of angels there,
To die for such as you.
He came down to a manger, came down to a world of sin,
Became a man and was crucified,
To save men from their sin.

From riches down to nothing, from praises down to shame,
A kingly crown to a crown of thorns,
That's why Jesus came.
No longer a little baby, now a Savior on a throne,
The King of Kings, praise to His name,
For sin He has atoned.

He was born as a baby in a manger, yes,
But Jesus was born to die.
It's sad that the world can celebrate Christmas,
Without ever asking why?

PEACE, BE STILL

(Mark 4v39 & John 14v27)

When the storm around you rages
And you're going through the mill
Remember the words that Jesus said
In the tempest—«Peace, be still»

In the middle of the turmoil
Of a busy life, we will
Often wonder if Jesus is with us
Then he answers—«Peace, be still»

If you're daunted by what is happening
And life seems a bitter pill
Struggling with problems and trials?
Jesus still says—«Peace, be still»

There is a way out of darkness
Better times just over the hill
Just remember when Jesus took control
And commanded—«Peace, be still»

His peace, He gave to help you
His peace, your heart can fill
If you'll only rest on Jesus
You'll find peace and you'll be still

You can trust in Jesus as Saviour
Let Him all your needs fulfil
Hear Him whisper softly to your heart
«I promised you peace. . .

                    Be still!»

PADDLING

Paddling in the shallows
Just dipping in!
Just up to my ankles
For that I'm thankful
It's far too icy
This will do nicely
For me

Going in a bit deeper
Just a little!
Just up to my waist
This is just to my taste
It's deep enough, for
The water's too rough
For me

Right in the deep part
I'm diving in!
Right over my head
I'll be bold instead, and
Let the water hold me
The deep enfold me
For Him

«Launch out into the deep. . .»
(Luke 5v4)

How many Christians are «paddling in the shallows» when the Lord wants them to be bold, for Him, and to trust Him and, in the words of Jesus', «launch out into the deep»?

PRAISE BE

Praise be to God the Father

Praise be to God the Son

Praise be to God the Spirit

Praise God the three in one

PSALM 23

(To the tune "St Michael")

The Lord, my Shepherd is,
I shall not be in need,
He makes me rest in pastures green,
By quiet waters, leads.

The Lord restores my soul,
He guides the path I take,
In righteousness He leads me on,
For His own great name's sake.

The Lord is with me now,
No evil need I fear,
For He, the Lord, will comfort me,
His presence always near.

The Lord sets out a spread,
For me, before my foes,
Anoints my head with precious oil,
And my cup overflows.

The Lord's goodness and love,
Is with me all my days,
I know I'll go to dwell with Him,
And be with him always.

SIXTY SECONDS

Sixty seconds every minute
It's amazing how fast that goes
Sixty minutes every hour
And then that hour is closed
Twenty-four hours in every day
Yearly, three sixty-five days
The same time available to each to us
The same time to use to God's praise
Let's make sure we use them
The seconds; the minutes; the hours
The days; the weeks; the months; the years
For they are God's—not ours

Make sure they're God's, not ours.

STAY CLOSE!

In the darkness in the rain—stay close!
In the storm and in the pain—stay close!
In the battle
In the confusion
In all of life's problems
He is the solution
In the uncertainty
Seek God's contribution
In all situations
Stay close!

THE BEST IS YET TO BE

When life is getting harder
And the way you cannot see
Remember, though the way be dark
The best is yet to be. . .

If you're feeling low in spirit
And downcast is how you feel
Lift up your heart and look to Him
The best is yet to be. . .

There's a future for the Christian
A heavenly goal to see
With Jesus as the centre and sun
The best is yet to be. . .

If you don't know Christ as Savior
From sin you're not set free
By asking Him into your heart
The best is yet to be. . .

(«the best is yet to be. . .» from a prayer by
Pastor Wesley Crawford)

THE LORD OUR MAKER

The Lord our maker
The Lord most high
The Lord our shield
God will provide

The Lord my banner
The Lord my peace
The Lord Almighty
The one who heals

Faithful; forgiving
One who sustains
God of the living
Our glory; our praise

My help; my refuge
My light; my song
My rock; my strength
Only wise God

God of all glory
God of all grace
God of all comfort
Be in this place

THE LORD HAS PLACED BEFORE ME

The Lord has placed before me an open door
To see God's will so clearly—I can't ask more
I must go through it
God's command—I must do it
And go where Jesus leads!

The Lord has placed before me an open door
A world-wide view for me God has in store
No man can close it
For now I know it
Will take me where God leads!

The Lord has placed before me an open door
I'll need His strength around me more and more
His word, I will keep it
His name, I'll proclaim it
And go wherever He leads!

«. . .see, I have placed before you an open door that
no-one can shut. I know that you have little strength,
yet you have kept my word and have not denied my
name. . .» Revelation 3v8

TWO MEN

(Luke 18v9–14)

Two men went up to the temple one day
Two men went up to the temple to pray
A Pharisee and a collector of tax
One so holy, the other lax
Which prayer would the Lord listen to?

The Pharisee stood up, what would he say?
Himself the subject, he began to pray
God, I thank you I am not like others
Evildoers, adulterers, robbers
I fast, and give God a tenth!

The tax collector stood further away
Not looking to heaven, he started to pray
God, have mercy on me, a sinner!
He beat his breast, repentance inner
Was clear to God who listened

Two men went up to the temple to pray
One prayer accepted, and one turned away
The collector of tax went home justified
The other on his own holiness relied
It was clear which prayer God had heard

For every one who exalts himself
No matter their position, no matter their wealth
It's clear they'll be humbled by the Lord
But if you humble yourself before God
You'll then be exalted by Him

UPS AND DOWNS

Ups and downs
Ins and outs
Smiles and frowns
Fear and doubts
Joys and sorrows
Starts and stalls
All our happenings
God knows them all!

In seeking and knowing
Picking and choosing
Coming and going
Winning and losing
Standing and sitting
Ruffling and smoothing
Missing and hitting
Testing and proving

In all our ways
In all our days
In all we do
God cares!

WE GAZE UPON THE WINE

We gaze upon the wine that's crimson red,
And think about the blood that Jesus shed,
We look upon the bread that's set before us,
And from deep within us swells this chorus,
'Worthy the Lamb who was slain
Worthy the Lamb who was slain'
For sinners, Christ died,
For us, crucified,
He died
there alone,
For sin
to atone,
We'll remember
His death,
To our very last breath,
«Worthy the Lamb who was slain»

«We gaze upon this wine, crimson red.. . .»
from a prayer at the Lord's table

WHEN I PRAY

When I pray—I'm praying to the wall or the ceiling
When I pray—my sin gets in the way
When I pray—I so often pray with feeling
When I pray—I just don't know what to say
When I pray—my mind so often strays from God
When I pray—my faith is oh so weak
When I pray—I focus on my own ways—not God's
When I pray—I'm awed by others who speak
When I pray—I do so in my own strength
When I pray—I worry about not praying well
When I pray—I worry about my prayer length
When I pray—my aim is so often to please men

But
When I pray—I talk to God
When I pray—God is pleased
When I pray—It's God who applauds
When I pray—It's my heart God sees

WHY BOTHER?

Why bother with the poor
Why bother with the needy
Why bother in world
that's increasingly greedy?

Why bother with the good
Why bother with the bad
Why bother in a world
that's increasingly mad?

Why bother with millions
Why bother with one
Why bother with anyone
who's done what they've done?

Why bother with prostitutes
Why bother with AIDs
Why bother with people
who go their own ways?

Why bother with murderers
Why bother with thieves
Why bother with so many
who do what they please?

Why bother with fools
Why bother with pride
Why bother with hypocrites
who are rotten inside?

Why bother with Arabs
Why bother with Jews
Why bother with Gentiles
all with opposing views

Why bother with anything
Why bother at all
Why bother in a world
that's heading for a fall?

Why bother with rebels
Why bother with mankind
Why bother with sinners
. . . *for all these Christ died*

WHAT DO DONKEYS THINK ABOUT?

What do donkeys <u>think</u> about
When they're standing against a fence?
What are the things that fly through their head
Do they really make any sense?

What do donkeys <u>talk</u> about
When they're munching at the trough?
Do they talk about straw, hay and carrots
About never getting enough?

What do donkeys <u>dream</u> about
When sleeping in their stall?
Do they dream about past, present, future
Do they dream about anything at all?

I believe they think about Jesus
And talk about the time
They dream about so often
When Jesus took a ride

In triumph, into Jerusalem
Along a dusty road
With palms before Him waving
On a lowly donkey He rode

No gold encrusted chariot
No prancing Arab steed

An ordinary everyday donkey
Was enough to meet His need

Donkeys are not well regarded
Used for any old thing
But one day outside Jerusalem
A donkey carried a King!

So each time you see a donkey
Look closely at its back
You'll see a cross marked plainly
A reminder of where Jesus sat!

What do donkeys think about
When they're standing perfectly still?
I believe they're thinking about Jesus
And the day they carried a king[1]

1. This poem was inspired by passing a little donkey in a field each eve-
ning on the way home from work on a bend in the road up on the hill above
Gransha Presbyterian Church at La Mon in the Castlereagh Hills! Every time I
saw it, the donkey was standing perfectly still, not a tail flicking or even an ear
twitching. It started me thinking—and the following poem resulted!

WORDS

Words
Suddenly, from on high
Like water dropping
Into a still clear pool
Causing ripples, unexpected
Calmness suddenly affected
The status quo changing
Stillness rearranging
Words from on high

WORLDWIDE, OUR TASK

Worldwide, our task
Worldwide, our vision
Reaching the lost
Our God-given mission

Worldwide, the challenge
Worldwide, the need
We need to be sowing
Life-giving seed

Worldwide for Jesus
Worldwide for God
Light for the darkness
Spreading His Word